CONTENTS

EFFECTING CHANGE

On April 29, 1970, US president Richard M. Nixon got a wake-up call. It would change history. It came in the form of a note from his advisers. Their message was clear. The nation was in a pollution crisis. And the government was not ready to deal with it.

The advisers laid out details on the pollution. They provided numbers as evidence. Americans were

Pollution from cities, industries, and everyday people became a major concern in the early 1970s.

throwing away 100 million tires, 28 billion bottles, and 48 billion cans each year. The long-term effect of all this trash was unknown. Experts worried it could cause major problems in the future.

The advisers suggested creating a new department called the Environmental Protection Agency (EPA). Several existing agencies would join into a single unit. They would oversee the government's environmental policy.

The president followed the

recommendation. On July 9, 1970, Nixon announced his plan to create the EPA. The US Congress approved the plan. The government officially formed the EPA on December 2, 1970. It changed how the US government dealt with the environment.

The Agency's Inspiration

The history of the EPA began with a note from Nixon's advisers. But the agency itself credits its creation to Rachel Carson. Its website says, "[The] EPA today may be said without exaggeration to be the extended shadow of Rachel Carson. The influence of her book has brought together over 14,000 scientists, lawyers, managers, and other employees across the country to fight the good fight for 'environmental protection.'"

This book, *Silent Spring*, was Carson's most famous work. It was published in 1962. The book drew attention to the negative effects of pesticides. She singled out the pesticide DDT as especially damaging. People praised Carson's writing for its attention to scientific details. They also liked its exciting and

The power of Carson's words brought about major changes.

engaging style. She made science understandable for everyday readers. *Silent Spring* inspired millions to care more about the environment.

Response to Silent Spring

Not everyone agreed with Carson. Pesticide companies were particularly opposed to her. However, she had a powerful ally. President John F. Kennedy took her work to heart. He ordered an investigation into the issues she raised. Carson and Kennedy formed a partnership in the fight to defend the environment.

Carson and her book took center stage in 1963. In that year, two congressional hearings on pesticides

DDT

DDT is short for dichloro-diphenyltrichloroethane. The compound was first made in 1874. Scientists did not realize it was poisonous to insects until the 1930s. DDT was useful during World War II (1939–1945). It killed the insects soldiers encountered. It became a valuable tool for farmers. In *Silent Spring*, Carson explained how DDT was dangerous to ecosystems.

Carson's devotion to protecting the environment inspired millions of people to think more carefully about the human impact on the planet.

were held. At the same time, Kennedy's own science committee agreed with Carson's call to restrict pesticides. By 1970 legislation would go into effect to protect the environment. Some new laws guarded endangered species. Others created rules about air pollution.

Carson helped Americans see the environment as a delicate system. She showed that humans were a part of that system. Her stand to protect the natural world sparked an environmental movement that continues today.

EXPLORE ONLINE

Chapter One begins by discussing the formation of the EPA. The website below also focuses on that topic. As you know, every source is different. How do the two sources present information differently? What can you learn from this website?

History of the EPA

mycorelibrary.com/environmental-movement

CHAPTER TWO

BECOMING A SCIENTIST

Rachel Louise Carson was born on May 27, 1907, in Springdale, Pennsylvania. She grew up on a farm near the Allegheny River. She enjoyed the natural environment around her home. Rachel explored nearby woods. She was especially interested in birds.

Young Rachel loved to write. She became a published author at age ten. A children's magazine

Carson maintained an interest in the environment throughout her life.

printed one of her stories. Her passions for writing and the environment would shape the rest of Rachel's life.

Early Environmentalism

Long before Rachel was born, people began thinking about the human impact on the environment. More than 2,000 years ago, people in ancient China, India, and Peru cared for their soil. Ancient Romans were concerned about water pollution. In the 1500s, people in Europe worried about pollution causing diseases.

But in the 1800s, people began thinking differently about the environment. Some people argued it should be protected for its own sake. The rapid growth of industry had increased pollution. People saw how wildlife could be harmed.

In 1900 the federal government passed its first legislation to protect wildlife. A law made it illegal to take hunted animals across state lines. Transporting some plants was against the law, too. In 1903

President Theodore Roosevelt created a national bird sanctuary. It was on Pelican Island in Florida. It was the first of 55 such sites.

At this time, John Muir was working to protect US lands from industry. The nature lover and author inspired Roosevelt. The president launched a program to conserve special areas. He created several national parks, including ones at the Grand Canyon and Yosemite. In 1924 the US government established the nation's first national

Roosevelt, *left*, and Muir, *right*, were two of the biggest figures in early US conservation efforts.

wilderness area. It was Gila National Forest in New Mexico. Wilderness areas do not have roads. They do not allow cars. Instead, visitors travel by walking or by riding horses.

Combining Science and Writing

In 1925 Carson began attending Pennsylvania College for Women. At first she studied English. Later she changed her major to biology. She earned her bachelor's degree in biology in 1929. Carson continued her studies at Johns Hopkins University. She earned a master's degree in zoology in 1932.

Next Carson taught zoology at the University of Maryland. During the summer she worked at a laboratory in Massachusetts. In 1936 Carson became an employee of the federal government. She took a job as a biologist with the US Bureau of Fisheries. This agency became the US Fish and Wildlife Service in 1940.

Carson's passion for writing continued. She wrote a series of pamphlets called "Conservation in Action." She published her first book, *Under the Sea-Wind*, in 1941.

R. L. Carson

While working for the government, Carson also wrote newspaper articles. She wrote about the environment for the *Baltimore Sun*.

Carson discussed pollution in Chesapeake Bay. She was credited as R. L. Carson. She believed that if readers did not know her gender, they might take her work more seriously. At the time, very few women were scientists.

The popularity of *The Sea Around Us* led to a movie adaptation and public displays.

In it Carson discussed birds and sea animals living on the East Coast. Carson received praise for her work. She presented scientific information in an easily understood style.

Ten years later, in 1951, Carson published *The Sea Around Us*. In this book, Carson showed readers the wonder of the world's oceans. She discussed their creation, their tides, and the animals that live in them. Carson's second title was successful with the public and critics. In 1952 Carson left the government to focus on writing.

Carson's third book, *The Edge of the Sea*, came out in 1955. It brought her increasing fame. This trend would continue in her next book, *Silent Spring*. It would skyrocket her into public view. It would draw the concern of citizens and politicians. It would also make chemical companies angry. *Silent Spring* would change environmentalism forever.

FURTHER EVIDENCE

This chapter discusses Carson's life leading up to writing *Silent Spring*. What is one of the chapter's main points? What are some pieces of evidence in the chapter that support this main point? Go to the article about Carson at the website below. Does the information on this site support the main point?

The Life and Legacy of Rachel Carson
mycorelibrary.com/environmental-movement

SILENT SPRING

BY
RACHEL CARSON

Introduction by
LORD SHACKLETON

Preface by
SIR JULIAN HUXLEY, F.R.S.

CHAPTER THREE

SILENT SPRING

I n her first three books, Rachel Carson showcased the beauty of the seas. She discussed the creatures that lived in or relied on them. Her fourth book was different. Carson used it to alert readers to the dangers of pesticides.

Carson did not initially plan to write about pesticides. She wanted her fourth book to be about children and nature. But a 1958 letter from her friend

Silent Spring helped spark the modern environmental movement.

DDT was widely sprayed on plants, animals, and even people in the early 1900s.

Olga Owens Huckins changed these plans. Huckins lived in Massachusetts and had a bird sanctuary. When DDT was sprayed in the area to fight mosquitoes, the result was a disaster. The chemical seemed to affect everything but the mosquitoes. Birds, grasshoppers, bees, and other insects died.

Huckins's letter returned Carson's thoughts to pesticides. Carson had been following reports about their effects. She knew they could be dangerous. Before beginning *Silent Spring*, Carson wrote to E. B. White, a journalist at the *New Yorker* magazine.

She asked him to write a story about pesticides. He could not take on the project. Instead, he suggested she should do it.

On April 1, 1958, Carson spoke with the editors of the *New Yorker* about the project. They agreed to publish her article, followed by a book on the danger of pesticides. The plan was to release the book in January 1959. The *New Yorker* article would appear first.

Researching the Topic

With her topic chosen, Carson set to work. She gathered facts. She sat in on government hearings about pesticides. She read scientific reports. She also interviewed experts, including doctors and researchers.

As she worked, Carson realized pesticides could be hazardous to humans. Her research convinced her that this should be the focus of the story. The pesticides were in widespread use by farmers, even though their long-term effects were unknown.

In the midst of work on her book, Carson faced major personal struggles.

The deadline of the book was pushed back. Carson realized she needed more time to investigate.

Personal Battles

On December 1, 1958, Carson's mother died. The personal loss pushed back the deadline again. Then, in early 1960, Carson developed pneumonia. In April she had surgery to remove two tumors. Her doctors sent her home.

Carson decided to get a second opinion. By the end of the year, doctors at another hospital diagnosed her with cancer. Carson started radiation treatment in early 1961. She kept her health issues secret as she worked on *Silent Spring.*

Completing the Work

Carson spent four years researching and writing. She began her book with the chapter "A Fable for Tomorrow." In it she describes a small town in rural America. She details a drastic change. Death strikes everywhere, from bees to birds to people. Even apple trees stop bearing fruit. Carson then reveals the cause: a strange white powder. She does not call it DDT, but she uses the powder as a stand-in for it and other chemicals. Carson then explains that although the town she described was not real, it easily could be. She also noted that each of the events really had happened somewhere. Finally she wrote, "What has already silenced the voices of spring in countless towns in America? This book is an attempt to explain."

DDT in fish-eating birds:
25 ppm

DDT in large fish:
2 ppm

DDT in small fish:
0.5 ppm

DDT in plankton:
0.04 ppm

DDT in water:
0.000003 parts per million (ppm)

Fewer organisms

More organisms

Bioaccumulation

Bioaccumulation occurs when toxic substances travel up the food chain. They become more and more concentrated at each step as organisms take in more and more of the substance. This diagram shows how bioaccumulation can quickly increase the concentration of toxic substances. How does it help you better understand how serious a problem bioaccumulation can be?

Carson went on to discuss how DDT moves through food chains. First, insects are sprayed with it. Birds eat these insects. The chemical enters their bodies. Carson explained that the chemicals do not always kill an animal. They may build up in its body.

The process is known as bioaccumulation. The chemicals can then cause problems later, harming the animal's offspring.

DDT is particularly harmful to birds. It causes the shells of a bird's eggs to be unusually thin. The thin eggs are unable to support the weight of growing baby birds. They collapse before the eggs hatch. This had a dramatic effect on bird populations. The American Bald Eagle was brought close to the brink of extinction.

In *Silent Spring*, Carson showed how life on the planet is related. Damaging one part of the environment harms other parts as well. Carson did not push for a complete end to pesticides. Instead

DDT Effects

Modern science has learned more about the effects of DDT since Carson's time. It can make nerve cells function incorrectly. These cells help the brain communicate with the rest of the body. But DDT can cause the cells to overload with messages and die. Exposure to DDT can lead to its buildup in a body. The chemical collects in fat tissue. It can cause tumors and damage the reproductive system.

she pushed for greater care in their use. She also promoted less harmful methods to control insect populations. Carson was ready to begin showing her work to the public. The first glimpse people would get would be her *New Yorker* article.

Approval

Carson's work appeared in the *New Yorker* in June 1962. The article spurred public interest. Ahead of the book's September release, people ordered 190,000 copies. US Supreme Court Justice William O. Douglas was a big supporter of *Silent Spring*. He read a copy of the book before it became available to the public. He wrote, "This book is the most important chronicle of this century for the human race. This book is a call for immediate action and for effective control of all merchants of poison."

Carson also got support from newspapers and politicians. The *New York Times* ran two stories supporting Carson. President Kennedy discussed Carson's book in a news conference. He said that

Justice Douglas provided important support to Carson's message.

because of the book, the government was looking into the dangers of pesticides. The following day, Kennedy made another announcement. He formed a committee to further explore the use of pesticides. All of this took place before the book was published. When *Silent Spring* came out, it received a new round of feedback. Not all of it was positive.

Backlash

The nation's major chemical companies tried to sue Carson, her book publisher, and the *New Yorker*.

When this failed, the companies spread negative publicity about Carson. They spent $250,000 trying to discredit her work. They failed again. One organization attacked the president for supporting Carson.

Many people used Carson's gender as an excuse to attack her. Some questioned her intelligence. They claimed she was being too emotional and sentimental. Others suggested she was overreacting. But critics could not make Carson or *Silent Spring* go away. She had made an impact on the public. Her message would grow over time.

An article from the environmental group the Natural Resources Defense Council includes a quote from Carson about humanity's relationship with nature:

> Carson was well aware of the larger implications of her work. Appearing on a CBS documentary about Silent Spring *shortly before her death from breast cancer in 1964, she remarked, "Man's attitude toward nature is today critically important simply because we have now acquired a fateful power to alter and destroy nature. But man is a part of nature, and his war against nature is inevitably a war against himself. [We are] challenged as mankind has never been challenged before to prove our maturity and our mastery, not of nature, but of ourselves."*

Source: *"The Story of* Silent Spring.*" Natural Resources Defense Council. Natural Resources Defense Council, December 5, 2013. Web. Accessed August 6, 2015.*

Point of View

Carson is arguing that when people destroy nature, they are really destroying themselves. Based on what you have read about Carson, why might she hold that point of view? What evidence from Chapter Three supports her argument?

CHAPTER FOUR

CARSON'S LEGACY

On May 15, 1963, President Kennedy's committee released a report called "The Use of Pesticides." In it the group demanded limitations on toxic chemicals. On June 4, Carson spoke to members of Congress about pesticides. She recommended the government create a group to address the issue. She suggested decisions

When she spoke to members of Congress, Carson urged them to limit the damage done by pesticides.

should be made with the public in mind, rather than businesses.

As Carson continued to fight for the environment, she also fought cancer. She limited her appearances to important ones. She focused on her treatment. It sapped her energy and strength. Finally, after fighting cancer for years, Carson died on April 14, 1964. She was 56 years old. She was gone, but her influence would continue for decades.

Carson's final book, *The Sense of Wonder*, was published after her death. In the book, she writes about the beauty of nature. She explains why the environment deserves protection. Carson wrote the book for her adopted son. She believed that the younger generation needed to be inspired to protect the planet.

A New Environmentalism

Carson's work sparked a new environmentalism. Muir and others promoted conservation. They wanted to maintain the nation's wild regions. Carson sent

1900

The Lacey Act, which makes taking animals killed by hunters across state lines illegal, is the first legislation to protect wildlife.

1963

The Clean Air Act becomes the first federal law to address controlling air pollution.

1965

The Water Quality Act requires individual states to create standards for water quality.

1970

The National Environmental Policy Act establishes national environmental goals and rules, including that federal departments determine how the government itself is affecting the environment.

1972

The Environmental Protection Agency bans DDT on June 14.

1972

The Clean Water Act restricts the amount of raw sewage and other contaminants that enter streams, rivers, and lakes.

1973

The Endangered Species Act seeks to keep animals and plants from becoming extinct.

Environmental Legislation Timeline

This timeline shows major environmental legislation passed between 1900 and the 1970s. Based on what you have read, which laws are most closely related to Carson's work? How many of them were passed after her death?

environmental work in a new direction. Through *Silent Spring*, she showed how humans are a part of nature. She said that all areas of the environment needed protection.

The federal government responded with new laws. President Kennedy, Carson's supporter, could not continue her work. He was killed in November 1963. Lyndon B. Johnson, his successor, continued to promote the cause. The first act he signed into law was the Clean Air Act of 1963. Johnson went on to approve several more environmental acts. They included the Water Quality Act of 1964 and the Air Quality Act of 1967. The year 1970 marked two important beginnings. That April the first Earth Day took place. The holiday calls attention to issues of environmental protection. Later that year, the EPA was formed. It was the organization Carson had asked Congress for in June 1963.

Silent Spring also led to the formation of many environmental groups. Greenpeace and Friends of the Earth are two major organizations that credit their beginnings to *Silent Spring*. Both groups continue to fight for nature.

Fifty Years Later

The year 2012 marked the fiftieth anniversary of *Silent Spring*. Today, Carson's message is part of everyday life. Many US companies and Americans now strive to be environmentally friendly.

More than a half-century since Carson's call for action against pesticides, the fight to ban such chemicals continues. The US government banned DDT in 1972, but other countries continue to use it. The United States has signed

Earth Day

The first Earth Day took place on April 22, 1970, in the United States. US Senator Gaylord Nelson organized the event with Harvard University student Denis Hayes. Millions of Americans showed their support for the environment. They wanted the government to protect nature. Hayes took Earth Day worldwide in 1990. That year approximately 200 million people in more than 140 nations participated.

On Earth Day in 1970, New York City's Fifth Avenue was closed to car traffic and filled with thousands of people.

international agreements to limit the use of harmful pesticides.

Writer, Scientist, Environmentalist, Inspiration

Many words describe Rachel Carson. She was a nature lover and a biologist. She was a writer, a teacher, and a mother. She was a passionate advocate for the environment. Together, these things made her a pioneer. *Silent Spring* did more than draw attention to the issue of pesticides. Her work changed the way the United States uses these and other chemicals.

Because of Carson's book, caring for the environment is an important goal in our society. Dozens of organizations carry on her fight to care for the natural world. They protect the air, the land,

PERSPECTIVES
An Unfounded Health Scare?

Silent Spring continues to be criticized. The American Council on Science and Health (ACSH) believes the uproar over DDT was unnecessary. This organization receives major funding from corporations. The council included *Silent Spring* in its 2004 report about "unfounded health scares." The ACSH said killing disease-carrying bugs was more important than DDT's impact on the environment. The ACSH cast doubt on the idea that DDT has negative effects.

Thanks to *Silent Spring*, Carson's efforts to teach people about the environment extended far beyond her death.

and the seas. Rachel Carson was a skilled researcher and had a gift for words. She combined these talents to spark the modern environmental movement.

On June 18, 2015, Pope Francis, the head of the Catholic Church, called for global environmental protection:

> Account must also be taken of the pollution produced by residue, including dangerous waste present in different areas. Each year hundreds of millions of tons of waste are generated, much of it non-biodegradable, highly toxic and radioactive, from homes and businesses, from construction and demolition sites, from clinical, electronic and industrial sources. The earth, our home, is beginning to look more and more like an immense pile of filth. In many parts of the planet, the elderly lament that once beautiful landscapes are now covered with rubbish. Industrial waste and chemical products utilized in cities and agricultural areas can lead to bioaccumulation in the organisms of the local population, even when levels of toxins in those places are low. Frequently no measures are taken until after people's health has been irreversibly affected.

Source: Pope Francis. "Encyclical Letter Laudato Si' of the Holy Father Francis on Care for Our Common Home." Vatican. Liberia Editrice Vaticana, n.d. Web. Accessed June 30, 2015.

What's the Big Idea?

Pope Francis is using evidence to support a point. Write a paragraph describing the point he is making. Include two or three pieces of evidence he uses to make that point.

IMPORTANT DATES

1907

Rachel Carson is born on May 27 in Springdale, Pennsylvania.

1929

Carson earns a bachelor's degree in biology.

1932

Carson earns a master's degree in zoology.

1955

Carson publishes *The Edge of the Sea*, her third book.

1958

On April 1, Carson agrees to write the book *Silent Spring*.

1962

The New Yorker runs the "Silent Spring" piece as a series in June.

1936

Carson begins working for the US Bureau of Fisheries as an aquatic biologist and later serves as editor of the agency's publications.

1941

Carson publishes her first book, *Under the Sea-Wind*.

1951

Carson publishes her second book, *The Sea Around Us*, which becomes a bestseller and earns her a National Book Award.

1962

Houghton Mifflin publishes the book *Silent Spring* on September 27.

1963

Carson appears before the US Congress on June 4 to discuss how the US government might deal with pesticides in the environment.

1964

On April 14, Carson dies.

STOP AND THINK

Say What?

Understanding the environment and pesticides means learning a lot of new vocabulary. Find five words in this book that you have never heard before. Use a dictionary to find out what they mean. Next, write the meanings in your own words, and use each word in a new sentence.

Tell the Tale

Chapter Three of this book discusses Carson's writing of *Silent Spring* and her experience with critics of her book. Write 200 words that tell the story of her experience. What did Carson do to learn about pesticides? What obstacles did she encounter? Be sure to set the scene, develop a sequence of events, and offer a conclusion.

Surprise Me

Chapter Two discusses Carson's experiences as a scientist. After reading this book, what two or three facts about her life in science did you find most surprising? Write a few sentences about each fact. Why did you find them surprising?

Why Do I Care?

Carson set herself up for attack by chemical companies and others by studying and writing about the effects of pesticides on the environment. How do pesticides affect your life? What effect might they have on you or the world?

GLOSSARY

bioaccumulation
the process of chemicals moving up the food chain and building up in the bodies of plants and animals

biology
the study of life and living things

endangered
at risk of becoming extinct

pamphlet
a small book about a single topic

pesticide
a chemical people use to kill bugs or animals that harm plants

pneumonia
an illness that affects the lungs and makes breathing difficult

sanctuary
a protected area or safe place

zoology
the study of animals

LEARN MORE

Books

Carson, Rachel. *Silent Spring*. New York: Houghton Mifflin, 2002.

Souder, William. *On a Farther Shore: The Life and Legacy of Rachel Carson*. New York: Broadway Books, 2012.

Websites

To learn more about Great Moments in Science, visit **booklinks.abdopublishing.com**. These links are routinely monitored and updated to provide the most current information available.

Visit **mycorelibrary.com** for free additional tools for teachers and students.

INDEX

ABOUT THE AUTHOR

Rebecca Rowell has put her degree in publishing and writing to work as an editor and as an author, working on dozens of books. Recent topics as an author include Marie Curie, Sylvia Earle, and ancient India. She lives in Minneapolis, Minnesota.